∞

Wake Up & Live!

How To Conquer The "Rip Van Winkle" Syndrome

Wake Up & Live!

How To Conquer The "Rip Van Winkle" Syndrome

Argus Gray

Disillusionment Press
USA / WORLDWIDE

Copyright © 2016 by Argus Gray

Original Copyright © 1998

ISBN-13: 978-0692655986 (Disillusionment Press)

ISBN-10: 0692655980

for all those who
have helped me to awaken

Introduction

This is a book of averages.
And though, while none of us fit
exactly into the mold of an average person,
we can all undoubtedly find a semblance
of ourselves in the usual descriptions.

The idea for this book hit me one evening as I stood in line at my local grocery store. I'm not a big stockpiler, so I often found myself shopping every other day, just buying enough for the next day or two—keeps things fresh I always justified.

As I waited in line I began to wonder how much time I actually spent shopping. As my mind began to calculate the minutes, into hours, into days; I was horrified by my rough calculation. Yes, granted this was my favorite market for buying groceries, not to mention the bakery selections were top notch, I still shuddered at the thought of how much of my life would be spent there.

I proceeded home and broke out the calculator. Perhaps I had miscalculated, but no—again and again, the sum was the same. Still, somehow I found it hard to believe. I knew because of my peculiar shopping method I frequented the grocery more than the average person, but I wasn't a big mall shopper so it had to average out.

S oon I was calculating the time I spent driving to work, talking on the phone, going to the bathroom. It seemed never ending. A substantial part of my life was being used up merely from the repetition of mundane utilitarian acts.

Suddenly, I realized I hadn't even factored sleep into my life. When I stared back at the astronomical number glowing from the calculator I felt myself slipping into shock. Even Rip Van Winkle had only slept for twenty years.

This was unbelievable! Why hadn't anybody told me about this? Surely I couldn't be the first person to sit down and tabulate these simple figures. It had to be a conspiracy, nothing this mind-boggling could ever be kept under wraps without a conspiracy.

Still, how could I have been so ignorant to the fact that the minutes of my life were slipping by like proverbial grains of sand through an hourglass?

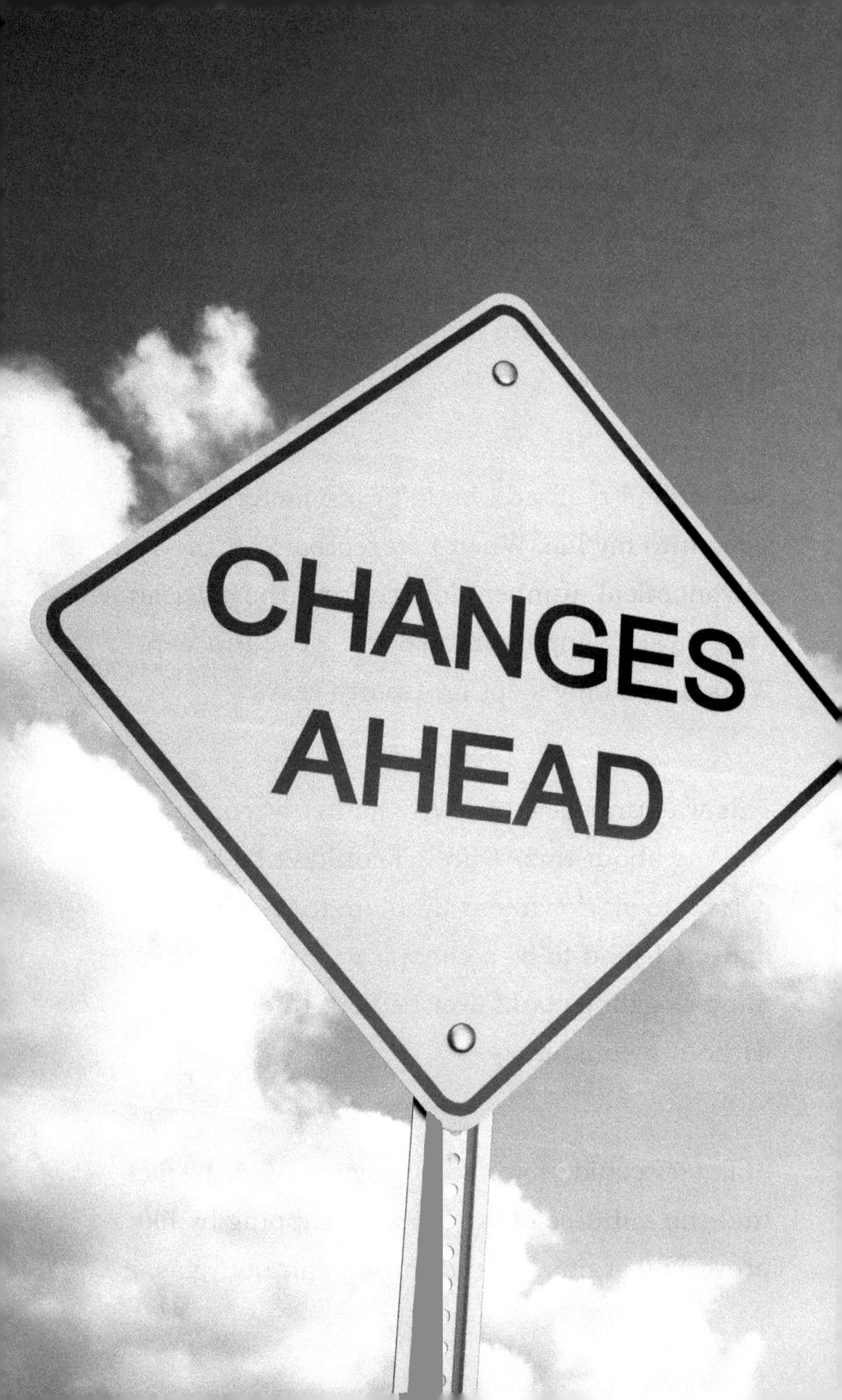
CHANGES
AHEAD

How often had I thought about doing something worthwhile only to put it off for later? How many times had I procrastinated; thinking, "Oh I have plenty of time, I'll do it tomorrow, next week, next month, next year."

For whatever reason, while I was living—no make that more like existing— in the humdrum routine of my day to day, I was completely oblivious to how precious each moment was that made up that very day.

I had forgotten to be grateful.

It was then I knew something had to change!

Part I

The Calculations

If you live
to the age of
75 ...

.. and, sleep 8 hours a day ...

you will be asleep for 25 years.

If you take a half hour for breakfast,

a half hour for lunch,

and an hour for dinner ...

you will spend 6.25 years eating.

If your education includes K-12,

then onto 4 years of college ...

you will spend 2.5 years in school.

If you are employed

from the ages of 20 to 65,

work 8 hours a day,

5 days a week,

50 weeks a year ...

you will spend 10.25 years working.

If you take a half hour to get up and ready in the morning, and another half hour to get ready for bed at night ...

you'll be getting ready for 3.1 years.

If you commute 45 minutes
each way for work…

you will be commuting for 2 years.

If you spend an average of 2 hours
a day doing chores: doing laundry, dishes,
mowing the lawn, washing the car, etc. ...

you will be doing chores for 6.25 years.

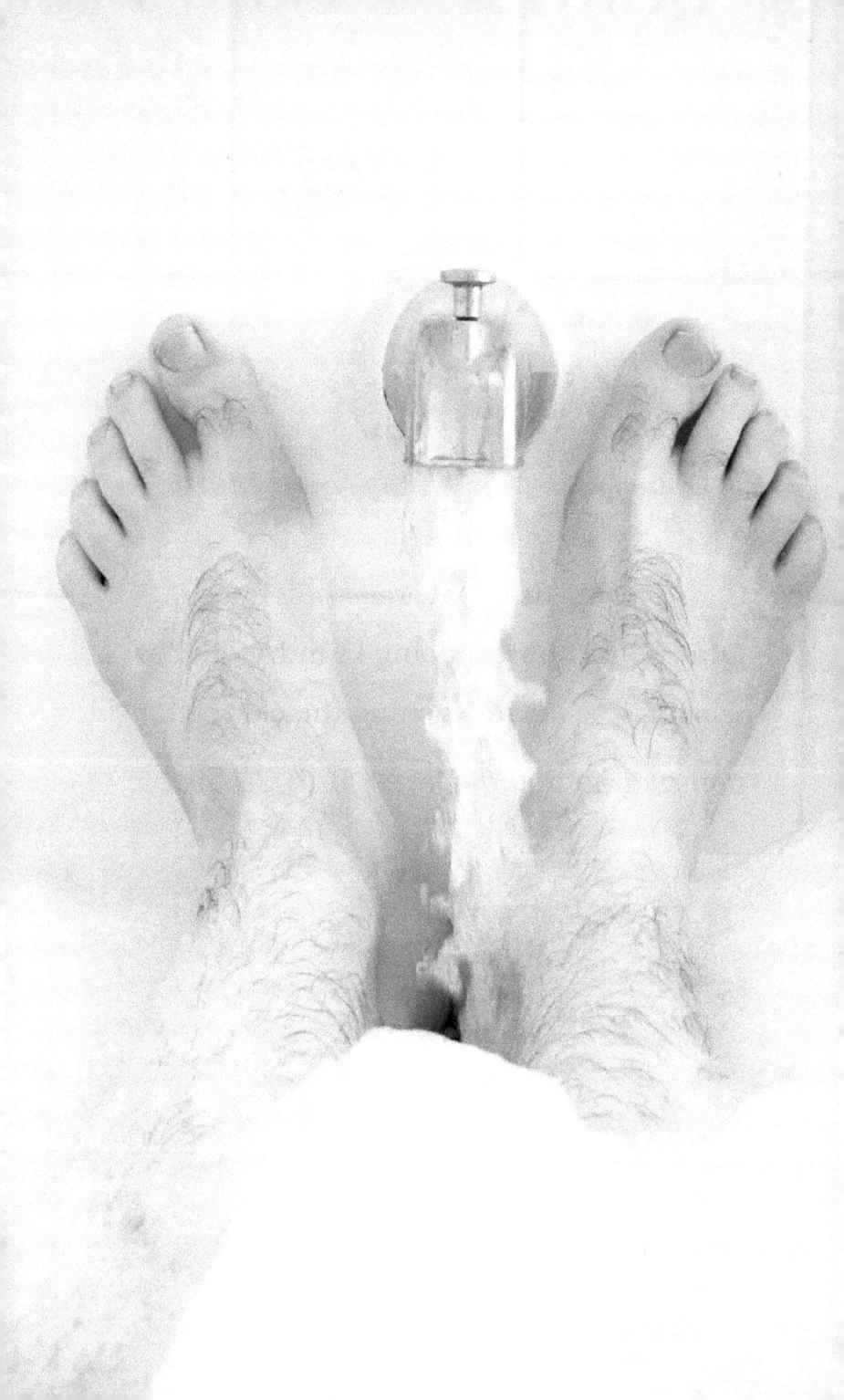

If you spend 20 minutes a day
in either the bathtub or shower ...

you will be bathing for 1 year.

Sitting in front of a television
(or a computer) 4 hours a day ...

will cost you 12.5 years.

If you average 3 hours a week shopping: for groceries, household goods, clothing, electronics, incidentals, etc. ...

you will be shopping for 1.3 years.

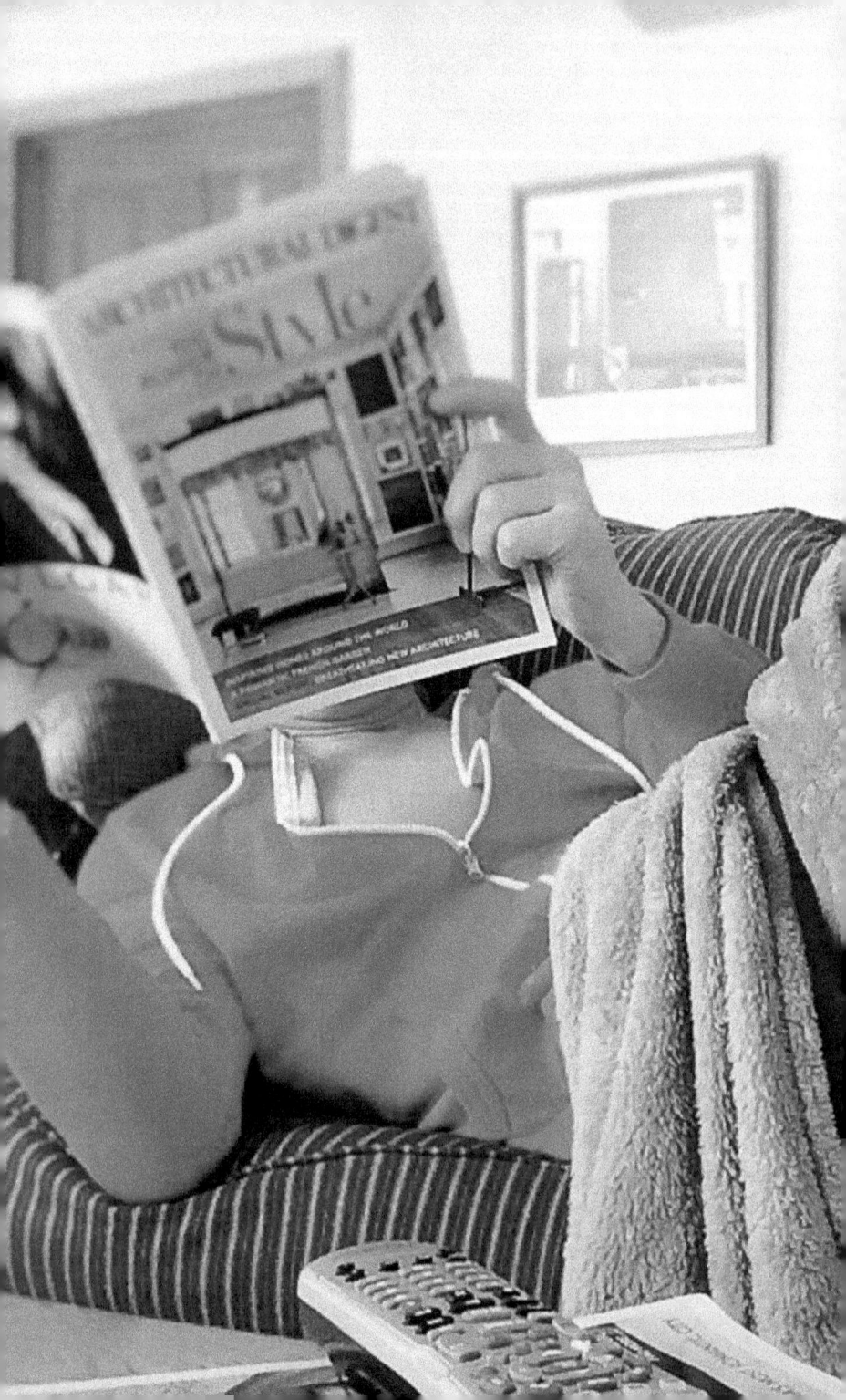

If you spend 1 hour a day for entertainment: reading, playing games, walking in the park, enjoying your pets, working out, etc. ...

you will be entertained for 3.1 years.

Part II

The Total

If you live to the age of 75 you will spend ...

25 years — Sleeping

6.25 years — Eating

2.5 years — Schooling

10.25 years — Working

3.1 years — Getting Ready

2 years — Commuting

6.25 years — Chores

1 year — Bathing

12.5 years — Television/Computer

1.3 years — Shopping

3.1 years — Entertainment

73.25 years

A BAD
HAIRDAY

New
Coffee Cup
(order)

S ubtract the total of 73.25 years from the projected 75 year life span, and what remains is a mere 1.75 years. That amounts to roughly, one year and nine months to step outside of our day to day routines.

That averages out to be just 8.5 days out of 365 each year (not counting the occasional leap years) that you and I will have the opportunities to do something other than what has been described in the previous pages. Yes, 8.5 days out of 365!— That's only 1.75 years out of a 75 year lifespan!

It's utterly amazing to me, that we're simply going to sleep 25 years of our life away— 25 YEARS! Rip Van Winkle, look out!

Why hasn't anyone ever told us this? Would anyone really dare to procrastinate if they knew how extremely limited their time was? One day there will be no tomorrows, at least not in these bodies. But at least for now we have this day, this very moment ...

What are you going to do with it?

Part III

The Conclusion

STOP
Wasting
LIFE

Some things in life are unavoidable. We all have to sleep, eat, and most of us, without a trust fund or mega-jackpot lottery win need to earn a living. But no longer do these events have to go unappreciated. I immediately tried to be more conscious of how I spent my time.

One of the first things I did was change my line of work. No longer would I spend my limited resources of time in a career that felt more like drudgery than productivity. I was tired of dreading each day just to get that paycheck at the end of the week. If I'm going to spend 10.25 years of my lifetime working, it will be spent doing something I love; something that will benefit others.

Not every one could understand my decision, for they had long ago sacrificed the desire for creativity in exchange for a pre-determined weekly paycheck. They had come to believe that without it, they couldn't afford to be happy. But with my new found awareness I realized I couldn't afford to stay, because it's not just money that can be spent foolishly. Time wasted is the most foolish expense of all.

I no longer felt the desire to spend my Sundays watching the 1 o'clock, 4 o'clock, and 7 o'clock games. Three football games add up to almost 10 hours of television—that's 2 1/2 days of average T.V. viewing in just one day. I had better things to do.

I began to notice my life being lived. I chose to do things not just to entertain me; but to enrich me. I listened to more and diverse types of music. I spent less time in   the local grocery store, and more time in the local bookstore. As I began to write and draw again, I recalled how much I had enjoyed it as a child. Why had I ever let that go? Had I become so consumed by earning a living, that I had forgotten what I was living for?

My whole life was becoming sweeter. Lunch was no longer a meal to be wolfed down while on the run. Now, even if in a hurry, I would take a moment to be thankful for that food. A simple sandwich that would equal a feast to those less fortunate living on the street. At this very moment, there are men, women, and children living in this city that do not have enough to eat. I had never taken the time before to think about that. To realize how blessed I was not to be hungry. My simple sandwich had become a feast unto me.

I made some calls and spoke to my aunt who has spent many years helping the homeless. How incredible she is to have done this for so long, to give of herself, yet I had barely even noticed.

I volunteered some time and helped at the local mission. My first experience consisted of setting tables and helping serve the nightly meal. As a volunteer, I was thanked for my help, but strangely it was I who felt like I should be

thanking them. They had shown me another part of the city; not a part to be ignored or tossed aside, but a part to be cared for. They taught me it cost nothing to love.

And while on the subject of loving and caring, let me add this—friends and family are treasures not to be ignored or taken for granted.

My friends, who can not be distinguished from family, because of them my life has been made so much richer. Thank you for all the laughter and good times we have shared. And, thank you for being there when I needed you most.

And my parents. Each time I now see my mother and father, I am so grateful for their presence; for them being a part of my life. I love them for who they are, just as they have always loved me for who I am. Sure, we still have our differing views, but now, time is no longer wasted on arguing. God only knows, I have not made their lives any easier, but hopefully I have made them fuller.

This new understanding which had sprung from a silly thought standing in the 15 items or less line had changed my life. I had become cognizant of my living—the breathtaking beauty of a sunset, the glimpse of a smile from a passerby, a cool breeze on a humid summer day. My life's daily experiences were becoming more and more vivid.

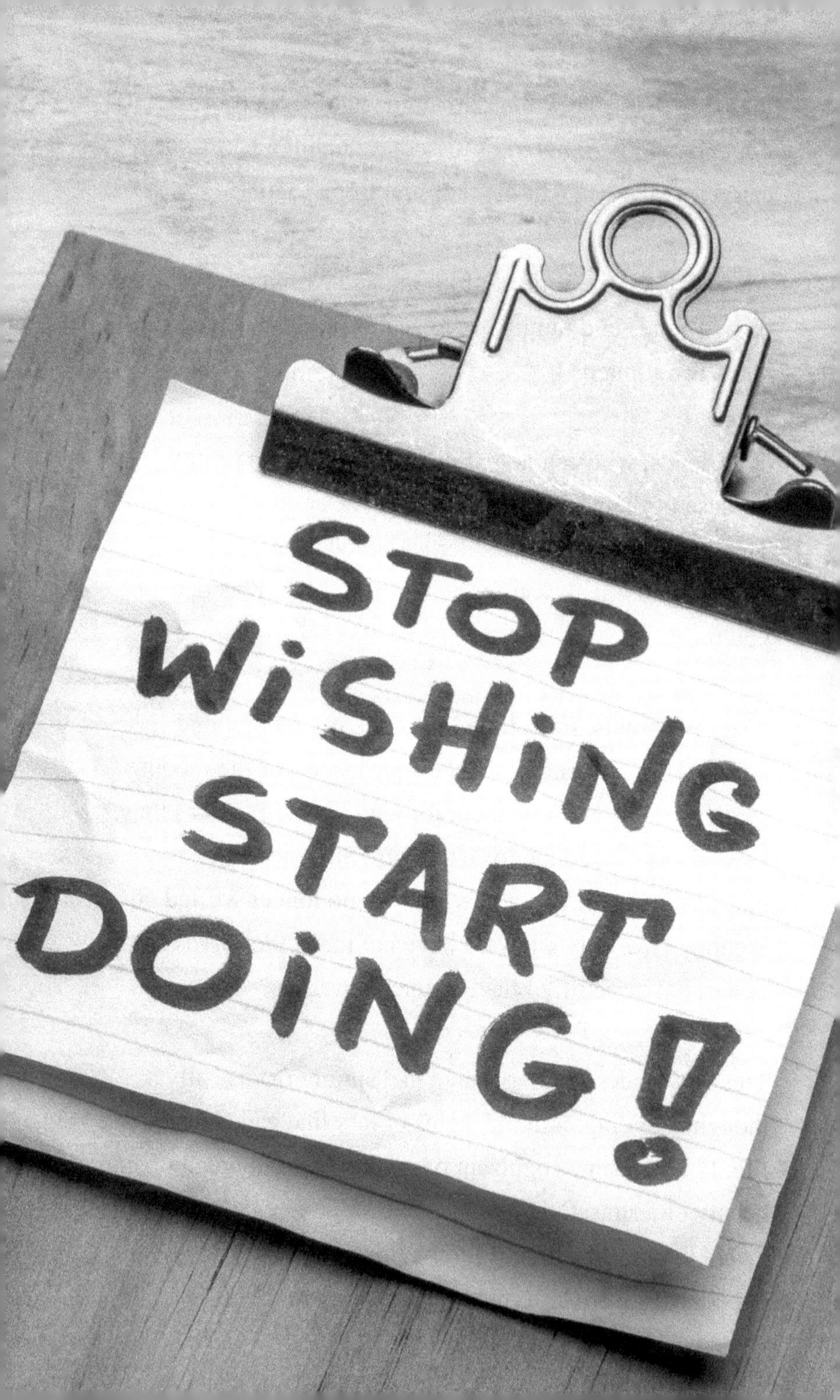
STOP
WiSHiNG
START
DOiNG!

But perhaps, the most fascinating aspect of all of this was though I now realized my time was extremely limited, I seemed to find more time than ever, to do the things I really enjoyed.

My life no longer consisted of mere minutes and hours— *it was now shaped by the moments and events of the day;* the people I'd meet, the meals I would have, and the simple acts of caring and kindness I could offer to those around me. Simply put, I had been asleep to the world, but now awake, I wouldn't waste the immense gift bestowed upon me.

I close with this wish. That you too, have been awakened; that this little book with its simple words has nudged you from your sleeping world.

There is so much you have to share. Don't be afraid, you are not alone. Give of yourself, to your friends and family. Tell them that you love them. Offer your time and services to your community and make a difference in someone's life.

You have a gift; the gift of yourself. Don't be afraid to give it. When you do, you will find that you are the one, who has truly been blessed.

On the timeline of your life,
how will you spend your time?

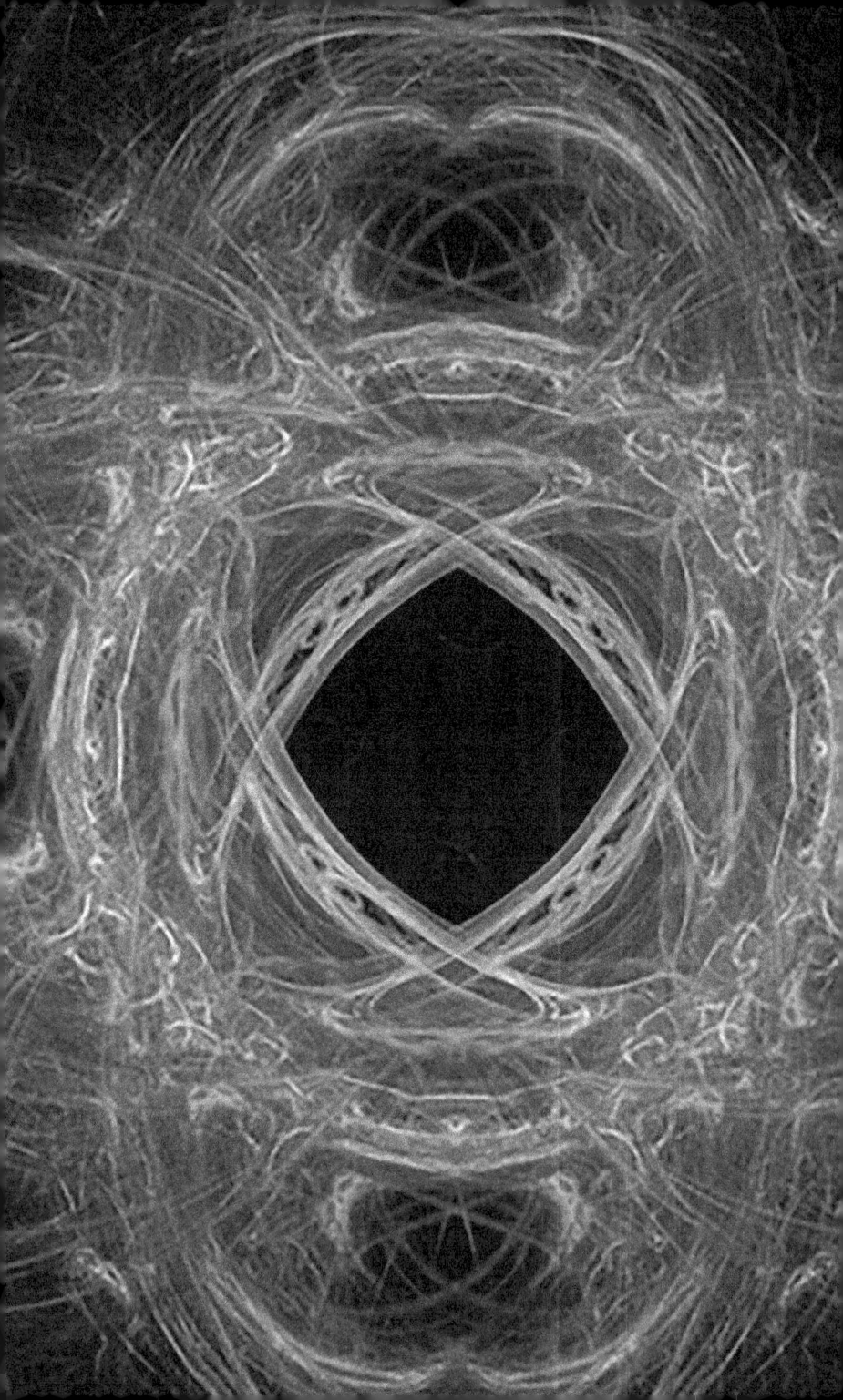

About the Author

Argus Gray is the name given to
a boy who has never grown up.

Whether it's because he can't ...
or because he won't ... is still unknown.

His physical body resides in Upstate NY,
driving his beautiful wife, Lenore, nuts from
his A.D.D. and erratic mood swings.

The rest of him ...
lives happily in his own small mind ...

.. writing quick read books for an A.D.D. generation,
and telling stories to whoever will listen.

Also by Argus Gray

Did You Know "Richard Cory"?

Who Am I?
A Simple Riddle That When Solved Answers
the Age Old Question We All Ask Ourselves…

Suicidal Thoughts

The Book of Truth
.. And Lies

If I Could Travel Through Time

Do You Know…
7 Simple Thoughts to Help You Awaken

Rubber Rocketship
A Very Short Story of Love, Loss & Eternity

Sleeping In The Trees
The Secret World of Princesses & Princes

Contact Argus Gray at:

www.argusgray.com

argusgray@gmail.com

Watch Argus Gray online at:

www.grayatnight.com

YouTube Channel: GrayatNight

www.ingramcontent.com/pod-product-compliance
Lightning Source LLC
Chambersburg PA
CBHW071851020426
42331CB00007B/1951